my
Contented Baby's
RECORD BOOK

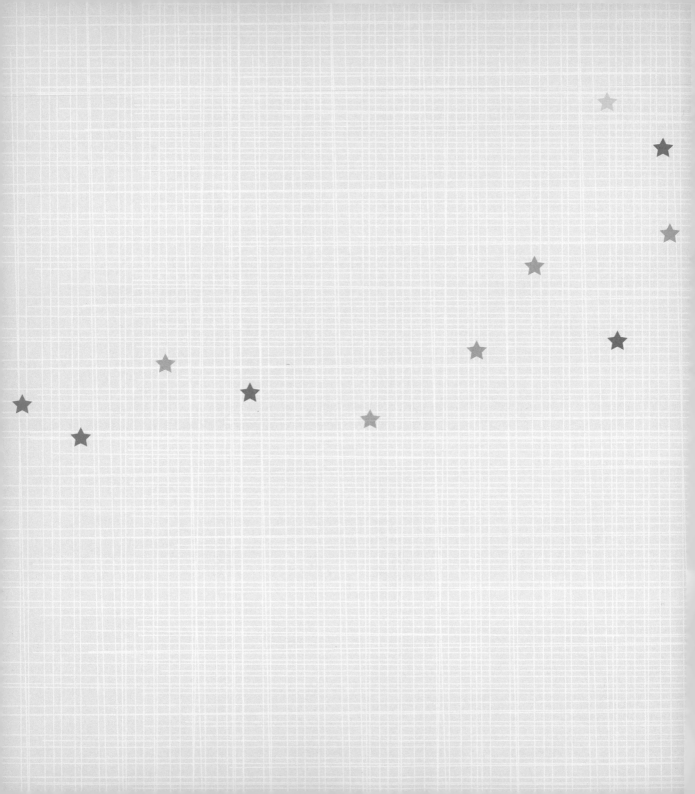

My
Contented Baby's
RECORD BOOK

GINA FORD

Vermilion

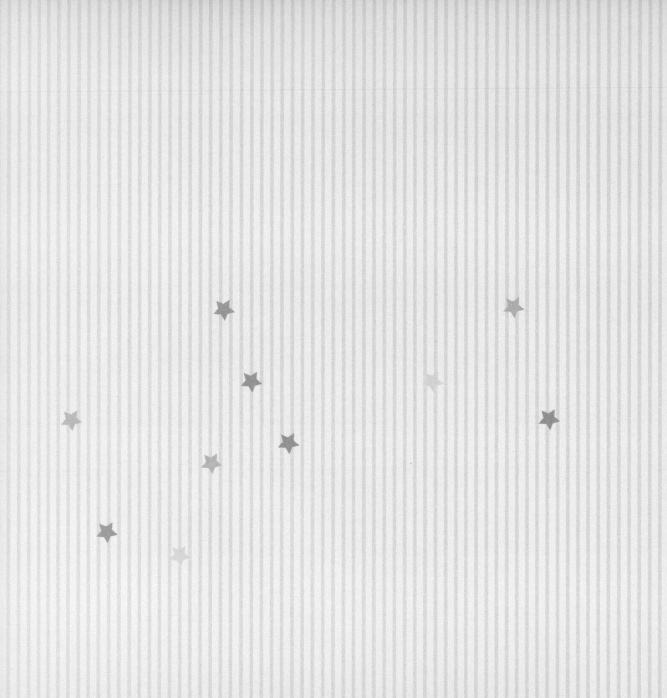

The first year can fly by, but this lovely book allows you to note down all the important milestones in your baby's development. Chart every detail, from the date and place of birth, the first smile, words and steps, plus your baby's routines, to the first birthday party. This will be a lovely memento for you to treasure the early memories of your contented little baby.

My story BEGINS

MY DUE DATE

....

MUMMY WAS IN LABOUR FOR

....

I WAS BORN AT

....

I WAS DELIVERED BY

....

DATE   DAY   TIME

....

WHAT MY
PARENTS WERE
DOING WHEN
MY MUMMY
WENT INTO
LABOUR
....

MY FIRST PHOTO

First APPEARANCES:

MY NAME
....

MY WEIGHT
....

MY LENGTH
....

MY HAIR COLOUR
....

MY EYE COLOUR
....

A LOCK OF MY HAIR

WHAT WAS HAPPENING IN THE WORLD

NUMBER ONE SONG

PRIME MINISTER

NUMBER ONE FILM

NEWS ITEM OF THE DAY

Coming HOME

I CAME HOME ON
....

THE CAR I WENT HOME IN
....

MY FIRST HOME WAS AT
....

FAMILY AND FRIENDS WHO CAME TO VISIT

....

PRESENTS I RECEIVED

....

My first NIGHT

WHERE I FIRST SLEPT

....

I FELL ASLEEP AT

....

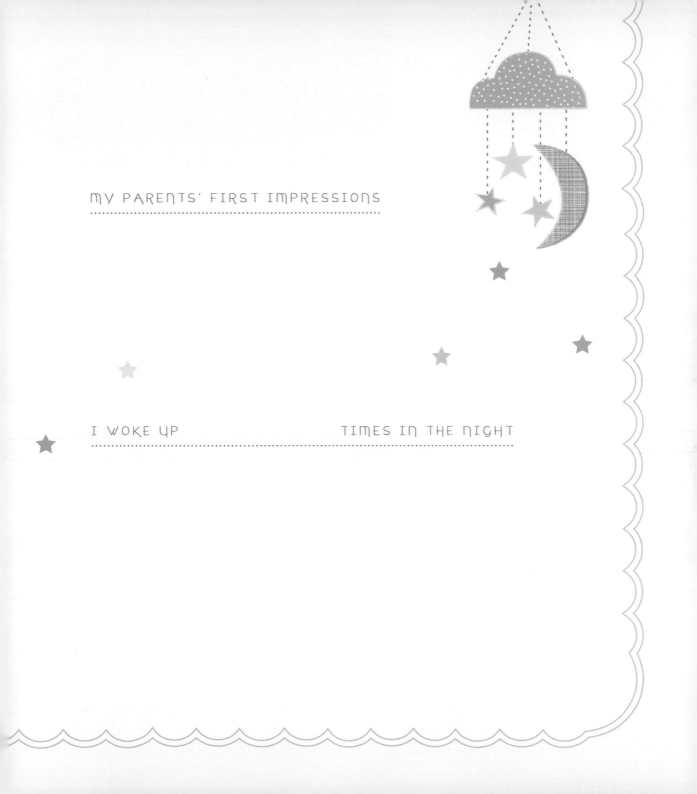

MY PARENTS' FIRST IMPRESSIONS

I WOKE UP   TIMES IN THE NIGHT

Birth to 1 MONTH

MY FEEDING AND SLEEPING ROUTINE
....

WHAT I LEARNED
....

PHOTOS

Birth to 1 month

MY FAVOURITES:

TOYS

....

ACTIVITIES

PLACES

PEOPLE

1 to 3 MONTHS

MY FEEDING AND SLEEPING ROUTINE

WHAT I LEARNED

1 to 3 months

MY FAVOURITES:

TOYS
....

ACTIVITIES

....

PLACES

....

PEOPLE

....

3 to 6 MONTHS

MY FEEDING AND SLEEPING ROUTINE

WHAT I LEARNED

3 to 6 MONTHS

MY FAVOURITES:

TOYS
....

ACTIVITIES

PLACES

PEOPLE

6 to 9 MONTHS

MY FEEDING AND SLEEPING ROUTINE

WHAT I LEARNED
....

6 to 9 MONTHS

MY FAVOURITES:

TOYS
....

ACTIVITIES
....

PLACES
....

PEOPLE
....

9 to 12 MONTHS

MY FEEDING AND SLEEPING ROUTINE

WHAT I LEARNED

9 to 12 MONTHS

MY FAVOURITES:

TOYS
....

ACTIVITIES

PLACES

PEOPLE

My Firsts

FIRST SLEPT THROUGH THE NIGHT

FIRST TIME I LAUGHED

FIRST SAT UP

FIRST TOOTH

FIRST WORD

FIRST SONG

FIRST PET

FIRST CRAWL

FIRST STEPS

FIRST PAIR OF SHOES

Food

SOLIDS INTRODUCED

....

FIRST SOLID FOOD

....

FAVOURITE FOOD

....

FOODS I DISLIKE

....

FIRST SAT IN A HIGHCHAIR
....

FIRST DRANK FROM A CUP
....

FIRST ATE FROM A SPOON
....

FIRST FED MYSELF
....

Bath TIME

GAMES IN THE BATH

MY FAVOURITE BATH TOY

BATH TIME PHOTOS

Naming CEREMONY

MY CHRISTENING/NAMING CEREMONY WAS ON
....

I WAS NAMED
....

IT WAS HELD AT
....

PHOTOS & INVITATION

Naming CEREMONY

FAMILY AND FRIENDS WHO JOINED US

PRESENTS I RECEIVED

1st CHRISTMAS

MY FIRST CHRISTMAS WAS SPENT AT

....

FAMILY AND FRIENDS WHO JOINED US

....

PRESENTS I RECEIVED

1ST CHRISTMAS PHOTOS

1ST CHRISTMAS PHOTOS

1st HOLIDAY

MY FIRST HOLIDAY WAS SPENT AT
....

PEOPLE WHO WERE THERE
....

WHAT WE DID
....

MEMORIES
....

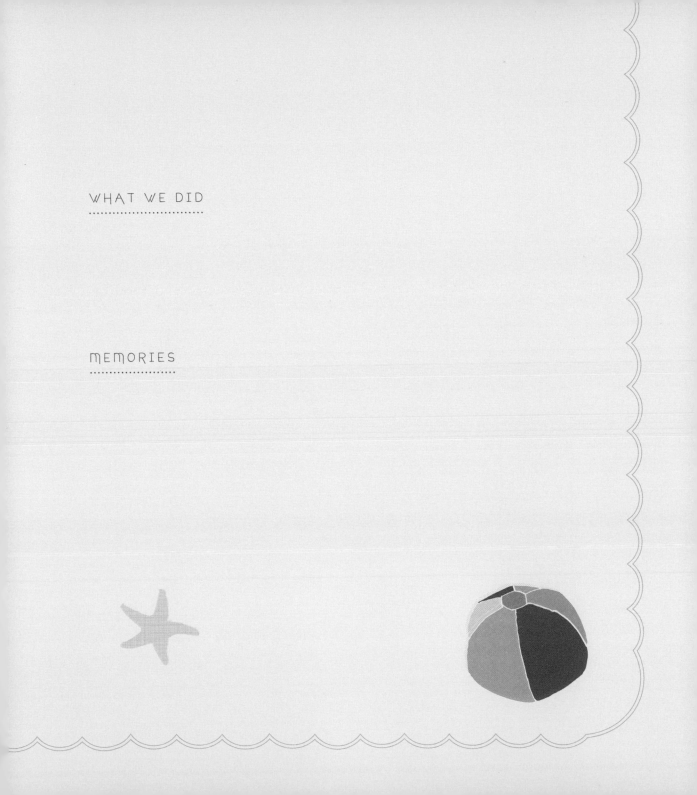

1st HOLIDAY PHOTOS

1ST HOLIDAY PHOTOS

1st PARTY

MY FIRST PARTY INVITE WAS FROM

....

PEOPLE WHO WERE THERE

....

1ST PARTY PHOTOS

1st BIRTHDAY

MY FIRST BIRTHDAY WAS ON

IT WAS HELD AT

FAMILY AND FRIENDS WHO JOINED US

PRESENTS I RECEIVED

1st BIRTHDAY PHOTOS

1st BIRTHDAY PHOTOS

Family TREE

GREAT
GRANDPARENTS

....

GRANDFATHER

....

AUNTS/UNCLES

....

GREAT
GRANDPARENTS

....

GRANDMOTHER

....

FATHER

....

ME

....

GREAT
GRANDPARENTS

GREAT
GRANDPARENTS

....

....

GRANDMOTHER

GRANDFATHER

....

....

MOTHER

AUNTS/UNCLES

....

....

BROTHERS & SISTERS

....

HEIGHT & WEIGHT

AT BIRTH
....

AT BIRTH
....

AT 3 MONTHS
....

AT 3 MONTHS
....

AT 6 MONTHS
....

AT 6 MONTHS
....

AT 9 MONTHS
....

AT 9 MONTHS
....

AT 1 YEAR
....

AT 1 YEAR
....

HEALTH

MY IMMUNISATIONS
....

MY ILLNESSES
....

MY BLOOD TYPE
....

ALLERGIES
....

HAND & FOOTPRINTS

3 MONTHS

6 MONTHS

9 MONTHS
....

12 MONTHS
....

10 9 8 7 6 5 4 3 2 1

Published in 2013 by Vermilion, an imprint
of Ebury Publishing

Ebury Publishing is a Random House
Group company

The Random House Group Limited Reg.
No. 954009

Addresses for companies within the
Random House Group can be found at
www.randomhouse.co.uk

A CIP catalogue record for this book
is available from the British Library

The Random House Group Limited
supports the Forest Stewardship Council®
(FSC®), the leading international forest-
certification organisation. Our books
carrying the FSC label are printed on
FSC®-certified paper. FSC is the only
forest-certification scheme supported by
the leading environmental organisations,
including Greenpeace. Our paper
procurement policy can be found at
www.randomhouse.co.uk/environment

Design and art direction by Georgia Vaux

Printed and bound in China by Toppan
Leefung

ISBN: 9780091947378

Copies are available at special rates
for bulk orders. Contact the sales
development team on 020 7840 8487 for
more information.

To buy books by your favourite authors
and register for offers, visit
www.randomhouse.co.uk